Conversations

on

Year of Yes

Shonda Rhimes

By dailyBooks

FREE Download: Bonus Books Included
*Claim Yours with **Any Purchase** of Conversation Starters!*

How to claim your free download:

1. LEAVE MY AMAZON REVIEW.
You Can Also Use the "Write a Customer Review" Button

2. ENTER YOUR BEST EMAIL HERE.
NO SPAM. Your Email is Never Shared and is Protected

Or Scan QR Code

3. RECEIVE YOUR FREE DOWNLOAD.
Download is Delivered Instantly to Inbox

Tips for Using dailyBooks Conversation Starters:

EVERY GOOD BOOK CONTAINS A WORLD FAR DEEPER THAN the surface of its pages. The characters and their world come alive through the words on the pages, yet the characters and its world still live on. Questions herein are designed to bring us beneath the surface of the page and invite us into the world that lives on. These questions can be used to:

- Foster a deeper understanding of the book
- Promote an atmosphere of discussion for groups
- Assist in the study of the book, either individually or corporately
- Explore unseen realms of the book as never seen before

About Us:

THROUGH YEARS OF EXPERIENCE AND FIELD EXPERTISE, from newspaper featured book clubs to local library chapters, *dailyBooks* can bring your book discussion to life. Host your book party as we discuss some of today's most widely read books.

Table of Contents

Introducing *Year of Yes*

THE NEW YORK TIMES BESTSELLING BOOK, *YEAR OF YES: How to Dance it Out, Stand in the Sun and Be Your Own Person* is Shonda Rhimes' newest book that dares everyone to say yes just as she did in her own life. This is a heartfelt personal account of a year where Hollywood's most powerful woman said yes and created significant changes in her life. If you love the stories in Rhimes' many groundbreaking television series, including Grey's Anatomy, Scandal, and Private Practice, this book will enthrall with its deep look inside the mind of the multi-talented and unexpected introvert, Shonda Rhimes.

She dominates Thursday nights on television with her eponymous company, Shondaland, which produces phenomenal shows that both entertain and intrigue viewers. These shows particularly feature stories of characters who are not afraid to voice their stark thoughts and live their lives the way they see fit.

But beneath this successful business figure lies a secret – Shonda Rhimes actually is a shy person. Her social anxiety was so severe that she needed to hire a publicist to evade appearing in public and would hyperventilate and panic every time she was interviewed.

Shonda's sister, Delorse, told her in 2013 that her entire behavior was focusing on never saying yes to anything worthwhile. This statement was the catalyst to this book. Here, Shonda bares everything she did when she dared to say yes to everything, even things that she had never done before because she was too afraid. From "Chapter 1: No" to "Chapter 15: Yes to Beautiful," this is a heartfelt chronicle of Shonda's journey. Her imaginative mind has loved books since childhood, which transitioned into her creating TV characters with lives and personas that starkly mirrored the daunting universe that she and everything she knew of lived in. She learned to overcome her fears, empower others through standing up for herself, and all the yes she needed to love her life.

Shonda Rhimes is an unexpected introvert but with her book, she shows how you can achieve your goals if you dare to answer yes to all that may challenge you, just as she did.

Introducing the Author

SHONDA HAS BECOME A BIGGER-THAN-LIFE PERSONA IN Hollywood today. As a great female presence in the show business, she has successfully cut a path for herself into popular and critical acclaim. Shondaland, her eponymous production company, which she has created, written, and exclusively produced to make it an efficient home to well-loved and sensational TV shows, including Private Practice and Grey's Anatomy. Her worldwide renown has earned her multiple awards and nominations, including but not limited to Golden Globe, Emmy, and Writer's, Producer's, and Director's Guild awards. Most significantly, *Time Magazine* recognized her contribution to the 21st Century as one of the 100 People Who Help Shape the World in 2007. Mainly a writer at heart (in part because of her introvert nature), she graduated with a Bachelor of Arts in English Literature and Creative Writing degree from

Dartmouth. She later finished her studies with a Master's Degree in Fine Arts at the prestigious USC School of Cinema-Television.

Her fame and successes mainly root from her bold brilliance in telling stories from controversial angles on social issues. She bravely created plots with characters cast against discriminative issues of gender, race, culture, society and religion – willing to risk criticism just to get her message shown. For instance, she took on the thought-provoking issues on abortion and took her stand, as we can see from how the female characters of some of her TV shows, including Cristina Yang of Grey's Anatomy, chose to abort their pregnancies because they did not want to have a baby.

Shonda Rhimes grew up in the outskirts of Chicago, Illinois. She now lives in Los Angeles with three daughters while she leads Shondaland, her own production company.

Discussion Questions

. . . .

question 1

Shonda was dared to say "Yes" by her sister. Do you think that the sister was a strong enough character to influence the changes that the protagonist (Shonda) had undergone throughout the story? Why or why not?

. . . .

· ·

question 2

Shonda wrote that she had never spoken without drinking at least two glasses of wine. Do you think that this was a good way to resolve the internal conflict she had (i.e. social anxieties)? Why or why not?

· ·

. . . .

question 3

The story is set in Hollywood. How do you think this affected the lives of the characters, especially the narrating protagonist, in the book?

. . . .

. . . .

question 4

Shonda, the protagonist, describes herself as the woman who has it "all" – financial success and single parenthood of three children. How do you feel about this particular description of the main character? Can you guess the possible emptiness in her that prompted the events of the story?

. . . .

. . . .

question 5

In the book, the protagonist cited her body weight as the fiercest
problem that she needed to confront. Do you think that this was
the best possible problem for her to confront in the story? What
else should be crucial problems within the story?

. . . .

. . . .

question 6

The story starts with Shonda telling the readers right away about her ability to lie easily. Do you think it was appropriate for her to do that? What else could she have said instead to start off the story?

. . . .

. . . .

question 7

In Chapter 2, Shonda admits that she is miserable. How does this admission prompt the crucial changes that she chose to do in her life? What other admissions could she have chosen to say and how would they have affected the story?

. . . .

· ·

question 8

Shonda said that she realized she did not die during a crucial
event in her life in Hollywood (i.e. talking on the Jimmy Kimmel
Show). What impact do you think Jimmy Kimmel had on Shonda
as a character in the third chapter?

· ·

. . . .

question 9

Chapter 6 was named, "Yes to Surrendering the Mommy War." Do you think that this was appropriate for Shonda to name the chapter as such? What else could be the name for this particular chapter?

. . . .

· ·

question 10

Chapter 7 is called, "Yes to All Play and No Work." How do you feel about this title? Why do you think Shonda chose this?

· ·

. . . .

question 11

Shonda recounts in Chapter 11 how she also learned to say NO. How much impact do you think this has on the progress of the story? Do you think that this was appropriate for Shonda to do?

. . . .

question 12

Chapter 12 introduces the reader to another supporting character in Shonda's story – her other sister, Sandie. She advised Shonda, "Gather your people." Do you think that this was an appropriate advice for the protagonist of the story to follow? Why or why not?

· ·

question 13

Shonda distinguishes herself in the story as someone who will find a different happy ending. How does this decision affect her character in the book? Do you agree with Shonda's version of a happy ending?

· ·

. . . .

question 14

The book ends with the chapter entitled, "Yes to Beautiful." Do you think that it was appropriate name for the conclusion of the book? What other titles could be used to clinch the end of Shonda Rhimes' *Year of Yes*?

. . . .

. . . .

question 15

The book's main theme is self-empowerment with a focus on female empowerment. How do you feel about the way this theme was shown throughout the book? Why do you think the author chose to focus her book on this?

. . . .

. . . .

question 16

Shonda Rhimes is a world-renowned creator who produced a
number of widely successful TV series including Private Practice.
If this book was written by another famous person, would it
enjoy the same success that Shonda Rhimes had?

. . . .

question 17

This book earned the award of An Amazon Best Book of November 2015. What do you think contributed to the success of this book?

. . . .

question 18

Aside from having a printed version of her book, Shonda Rhimes
also spoke in a TEDx event. Which appealed to you more: reading
Shonda Rhimes' own words or hearing them?

. . . .

. . . .

question 19

The New York Times called this a powerful book, worthy as a gift for one's self or a friend. Do you agree with this? Do you think that this is an appropriate gift from Shonda Rhimes to her fans?

. . . .

· ·

question 20

92% of Goodreads users like Shonda Rhimes' *Year of Yes*. Why do you think the remaining eight percent did not like this book?

· ·

FREE Download: Bonus Books Included

*Claim Yours with **Any Purchase** of Conversation Starters!*

How to claim your free download:

4.   LEAVE MY AMAZON REVIEW.

You Can Also Use "Write a Customer Review" Button

5.   ENTER YOUR BEST EMAIL HERE.

NO SPAM. Your Email is Never Shared and is Protected

Or Scan Above

6.   RECEIVE YOUR FREE DOWNLOAD.

Download is Instantly Delivered to Inbox

. . . .

question 21

Only 40% of readers at the online books site, Goodreads, rated this book with 5 stars. Do you agree with their assessment?

. . . .

question 22

Christina Haywood of http://wonderwanderonline.com deemed Year of Yes as February 2016's Book of the Month. Why do you think she chose this book?

· ·

question 23

Shonda Rhimes also wrote the screenplays for *Princess Diaries 2: A Royal Engagement*, *Crossroads*, and *Introducing Dorothy Dandridge.* How do you feel about the differences in reading her self-proclaimed memoir?

· ·

question 24

Women & Hollywood/ Indiewire.com describe the aftermath of reading this book as "having a new best friend" in their review. Do you agree with their description? Why or why not?

. . . .

question 25

LA Times tells in their review that reading this book is just as fun an experience as watching Rhimes' TV series. If you had watched one or more of Rhimes' TV series, what would you say about this book, now talking about Shonda's own life?

. . . .

. . . .

question 26

Shonda, the book's author, said that "Standing around like
Wonder Woman in the morning can make people think you are
more amazing at lunchtime." How do you interpret this
statement? Is this applicable to your daily life?

. . . .

. . . .

question 27

"I work to feed and clothe you. Do you want food and clothes? Then be quiet and show come gratitude." What can you glean from this particular quote? How do you feel about Rhimes' parenting methods?

. . . .

. . . .

question 28

Shonda wrote that even if many people dream, the real, successful, happy, and powerful people engage themselves in busily doing their work. What implications can be deduced from these words, especially about how the book's author imparts the knowledge? Do you agree with them?

. . . .

. . . .

question 29

Shonda stresses the tough work that motherhood is, especially
"lest [you] risk messing up another person forever." Judging from
your own experiences (be you a mother, child, or a father), do
you agree with Shonda?

. . . .

. . . .

question 30

Shonda uses a particular word, "badassery." What does this show about Shonda's work ethic? Do you find this applicable in your own life?

. . . .

. . . .

question 31

Shonda recalls the "I don't" reply she gives to those who asks her about how she does it all. How do these two words synthesize and aptly describe whatever difficulties in her life? What other answers do you think that the author could have given and how would that have affected the story?

. . . .

. . . .

question 32

Shonda recounts how she spent her high school trying to copy
Whitney Houston's characteristic curls, only to find upon her
adulthood that it was just a wig. How would you have reacted?
And, what would you do if you were in Shonda's shoes at that
point in time?

. . . .

. . . .

question 33

Introversion as a natural trait is clearly established within the lines in the book. How does this emphasis affect your opinion and knowledge about popular and powerful people? How would the book have been different if Shonda was an extrovert?

. . . .

. . . .

question 34

To Shonda Rhimes, the whole point of the "Year of Yes project" is to say yes to things that scare her. How do you think her life and the book would have been different if she did not take on this project?

. . . .

. . . .

question 35

Shonda explicitly said that there are no rules to finding happiness. Why do you think she said this? What would you do if there are no rules to happiness? How would the book have been different if Shonda had a list of rules to follow?

. . . .

. . . .

question 36

Shonda was asked to speak at the Commencement Ceremonies of her alma mater, Dartmouth and dared to say YES to that. If you were Shonda, what would you have done in that situation?

. . . .

. . . .

question 37

Shonda chose to be single, instead of getting married, because she wanted to have a different happy ending. What do you think caused her to such a decision and how did that change her life? If you were Shonda, how would you define a happy ending?

. . . .

. . . .

question 38

Shonda wrote that, "While a lot of people are busy dreaming, the really powerful and successful people are busy doing." Why do you think she said this statement? If you could talk to Shonda about your reaction to this, what would you tell her? How do you think Shonda's life would be different if she did not have this work ethic?

. . . .

Quiz Questions

. . . .

question 39

_____ said to Shonda, "You never say yes to anything."

. . . .

question 40

The book's main theme is _____ with a focus on _____.

question 41

In Chapter 2, Shonda admits that she is _____.

question 42

_____ advised Shonda, "Gather your people."

question 43

True or false: Shonda recounts in Chapter 11 how she also learned to say NO

question 44

True or false: Shonda did not tell the readers about her ability to lie easily.

. . . .

question 45

True or false: Shonda said yes to be a guest at the Jimmy Kimmel Show.

. . . .

question 46

Shonda Rhimes grew up in the outskirts of _____.

question 47

Shonda recounts in her book how she spent her high school trying to copy _____'s characteristic curls, only to find upon her adulthood that it was just a wig.

question 48

She graduated with a Bachelor of Arts degree in English Literature with Creative Writing at _____.

question 49

True or false: Shonda Rhimes is an introvert.

question 50

True or false: Shonda wrote stories with characters cast against stereotypes and underrepresentation.

Quiz Answers

1. Delorse, Shonda's sister
2. self-empowerment; female empowerment
3. miserable
4. Sandie, Shonda's sister
5. TRUE
6. FALSE – Shonda did tell her readers she can lie easily
7. TRUE
8. Chicago, Illinois
9. Whitney Houston
10. Dartmouth College
11. TRUE
12. TRUE

THE END

Want to promote your book group? Register here.

FREE Download: Bonus Books Included

*Claim Yours with **Any Purchase** of Conversation Starters!*

How to claim your free download:

7. LEAVE MY AMAZON REVIEW.
You Can Also Use "Write a Customer Review" Button

8. ENTER YOUR BEST EMAIL HERE.
NO SPAM. Your Email is Never Shared and is Protected

Or Scan Above

9. RECEIVE YOUR FREE DOWNLOAD.
Download is Instantly Delivered to Inbox